MW00710746

The *Reflection* of God

The *Reflection* of God

Tonya Heavin

TATE PUBLISHING *& Enterprises*

TATE PUBLISHING
& Enterprises

The Reflection of God

Copyright © 2006 by Tonya Heavin. All rights reserved.

No part of this publication may be reproduced, stored in a retrieval system or transmitted in any way by any means, electronic, mechanical, photocopy, recording or otherwise without the prior permission of the author except as provided by USA copyright law.

Scripture quotations marked "NIV" are taken from the *Holy Bible, New International Version* ®, Copyright © 1973, 1978, 1984 by International Bible Society. Used by permission of Zondervan Publishing House. All rights reserved.

The opinions expressed by the author are not necessarily those of Tate Publishing, LLC.

Book design copyright © 2006 by Tate Publishing, LLC. All rights reserved.
Cover design by Kristen Polson
Interior design by Jennifer Redden

Published in the United States of America

ISBN: 1-5988678-1-4
06.10.04

To Geoff, Kelton, and Brenna for being three perfect examples of how truly amazing God's blessings are in my life.

Acknowledgements

My family and friends have provided encouragement and support throughout this project. I am truly grateful for their generosity in reading and offering suggestions and for their continued prayers.

Kim Breen and Tori Ledbetter, thank you for cheering me on and offering constructive criticism. You have truly helped me grow.

Jan Colvin and JoAnn Chapman, God blessed me with one mom at birth and another mom through marriage. I love you both.

Kelton and Brenna, I am excited to see where our next adventures together will take us. You are both special, and I love you dearly.

Geoff, God knew exactly what I needed in my life . . . you!

Each day I am amazed at what He does in our lives. Thank you for sharing these days with me. I love you.

God, thank You for blessing me with the words to write of Your love and faithfulness.

Table of Contents

Foreword

A number of years ago a well-known author wrote a book declaring that all he really needed to know he learned in kindergarten. The truth is that our journey through life is filled with opportunities to learn, gain insight into oneself, and mature in our relationship with God. For more than a decade and a half I have watched Tonya Heavin grow, becoming in the process a delightful and dedicated Christian woman, devoted wife, and energetic mother. That Tonya is an educator encourages her to see more than many would. The fact that she is willing to reflect on her experiences with her children, Kelton and Brenna, and her husband Geoff, opens up a world rich with spiritual insight. Wise is the parent who realizes that raising children offers tremendous potential for growth. In the process of sharing her reflections, Tonya encourages all of us to be on the lookout for God in all of life's experiences. The end result is discovering God's delightful ways in revealing Himself through those we love the most.

—Bob Johnston, Pastor,
First Baptist Church, Rolla, Missouri

The Search

"What do you think? If a man owns a hundred sheep, and one of them wanders away, will he not leave the ninety-nine on the hills and go to look for the one that has wandered off? And if he finds it, I tell you the truth, he is happier about that one sheep than about the ninety-nine that did not wander off. In the same way your Father in Heaven is not willing that any of these little ones should be lost."

Matthew 18:12–14 (NIV)

One fall weekend afternoon, I decided to take my children, Kelton, then four, and Brenna, two and a half, to the local inside swimming pool for some water play. We had visited The Centre many times before so we had a routine established.

The pool had a child-friendly section which wound around to the deeper parts. In between the child portion and the lap swim area was a deep section where a large two story water slide emptied.

For obvious reasons we always stayed in the shallow, child-friendly section splashing each other. Another popular water play area was a large frog shaped slide. The tongue of the frog extended to the surface of the water. Brenna had just started going down the slide by herself. I would get out of the pool and follow her to the steps. She was then able to climb up the few steps, sit down and wait to slide down to me. I would jump back in the pool and be ready to catch her. I would catch her before she went under the water. Kelton was a pro at this. He could go forwards, backwards, on his belly and on his back.

After watching Kelton a few times Brenna felt independent enough to try it on her own that day. I lifted her out of the water and onto the side of the pool. She was going to walk around the frog slide to the steps, climb up and then slide on down to me. I stood in the water for her and waited.

I thought she was being stubborn and had decided to sit on the steps to the slide. I called out to her.

"Brenna, go on down the slide."

Silence.

"Brenna, let's go."

Again, silence.

A twinge of fear started to form. When I saw another child walk around the slide and go down, I jumped out of the pool. I glanced down at Kelton and instructed him not to move.

I ran the two steps around the slide. No Brenna.

I could feel my chest tightening. A mother's worst fear . . . her child lost at a public pool.

I started yelling her name. My voice sounded hollow in my head. I yelled again to Kelton.

"Have you seen your sister?"

"No, Momma."

I believe he could sense my fear because he immediately climbed out of the pool and grabbed my hand.

I felt, actually felt, my eyes darting, searching for a little two and a half-year-old in a fish swimsuit.

In that moment of panic I didn't know which way to go. The doors leading out of the facility were to the right of the slide. Could someone have grabbed her and left the building? It was in those moments that I remembered, or tried to remember every person I had witnessed when we had walked in thirty minutes earlier. The lady, the one with all the tattoos, who had been sitting by the doors, was no longer perching on the barstool. Could she have taken my baby? Looking back I know I had prejudged her, but to my frazzled mind I was desperate to find my child and grasped at whatever possible solution there could be. I remembered a group of pre-teens that had walked by the frog slide on their way to the big water slide. Could she have joined them? Another mother had been sitting close to the doors watching her children play. A quick glance showed she was still sitting in the same chair.

My other option was the pool itself. I found myself reluctantly searching the pool. Gripping Kelton's hand in my own I was nearly running up and down the side of the pool terrified of what I might find.

The mother who had been sitting by the doors caught onto my sense of urgency and hopped up to help search. I reached the point where all I wanted to do was to sit and cry. Instead I ran back around to the child play area of the pool and yelled at the lifeguard.

"I can't find my daughter. I can't find her. She's two. Please help."

The lifeguard started scanning the pool. Of course to my frazzled nerves and aching, worried heart, that wasn't enough. It all seemed to me to be happening in slow motion. But then I heard the words. They were words that I grasped onto with hope.

"Is that her?"

I followed the pointing finger of the lifeguard. On the heels of instant joy came instant fear when I realized her location.

My little girl was being held by two girls in the section of the pool that the water slide emptied into. The girls looked to be about nine or ten years old. As I started running toward them they were bringing her to me. As soon as I had my baby in my arms again I turned to the girls. I am sure my voice came across as harsh, but I needed to know the truth.

"Did you take her there?"

"No, no, we were getting her out."

I was torn—on one hand I was glad to know she was safe and they had helped her. However, I was also scared. How did she end up there?

I thanked the girls who seemed genuinely concerned. Refusing to let go of either of my children, I threw towels around them and left. By the time we got home shock was setting in. I couldn't stop shaking.

I was able to hold off the tears until I got the kids settled with a snack and I could hide for a few moments behind a closed bedroom door. Then the tears came. I cried until I could cry no more. I knew that what had just happened could have had an entirely different ending.

When I calmed down enough to talk, I called Geoff, my husband. My husband is a flight paramedic with a work schedule that takes him away from home quite a bit. It is a normal routine for our family to have Geoff gone for forty-eight hours at a time often several times a week. It is not the easiest schedule to deal with, but we all work hard to keep our family strong. When I called him that evening part of me was scared to tell him what had occurred that afternoon. I felt I had let him down by not being able to find our child. Another part of me needed the reassurance of someone who loved me and would understand without judging.

I did a lot of praying that evening, thanking God for keeping my daughter safe. It was later that night after I had replayed the afternoon over and over in my head that I truly started to see the correlation between my daughter who was lost to me and the shepherd who went out in search of one lost sheep. Ultimately, there is our God who wants no one to be lost.

It is easy to relate to a parent who is searching for a wayward child or one who is hidden from view for a period of time. The amount of time is inconsequential. Thirty seconds or thirty years, the sharp sting and the dull nagging ache of pain are still signals of loss.

It is even easy to relate to the shepherd in search of his lost sheep. How many people do you know search for a lost pet who is dear to the family, or the farm animal that has strayed from the herd? The importance, to the one searching, is strong— stronger perhaps for the one who feels personally responsible.

Think about our Heavenly Father who aches for each and every lost child, each soul who is searching for something. Something to take away the pain, the loneliness, the empty ache that consumes their hearts, their very being. God does what we are unable to do. He searches for the ones that we deem unlovable. He searches for the ones we shy away from. He searches for the ones we are scared of. He searches for you.

Try to imagine God's fear. Fear for the one who refuses to call out His holy name. Fear for the child who has never even heard His name. Fear for those who ache with a pain so intense, so deeply troubling that they feel as if they cannot take another step or voice a single word: Father.

I know that God was with my family that fall day at the pool. I may not ever know what all God did that afternoon to keep my daughter safe. I am forever grateful. I still have the chance to be a mother to a precocious, demanding, loving, joyful little girl. It is also with joy that I am able to say that I know and love a God who searched for me when I was lost . . . a God who searches, never ceasing, for each soul.

Father God, thank You for not giving up the search for me. Help me to realize that each and every person is special and worthy of Your unfailing love.

Gifts of Love

"*Every good and perfect gift is from above, coming down from the Father of the heavenly lights, who does not change like shifting shadows.*"

James 1:17(NIV)

"Please, Mom. Please, please, Mom."

All morning I had heard the same pleas. Kelton, five, and Brenna, three, wanted to go roller skating. It was one of those overcast spring days. No one wanted to stay in the house yet it was a bit too damp to play in the backyard.

Finally, after lunch and nonstop pleading, I agreed we could go skating. Our skating rink also houses a play area with all types of climbing and jumping apparatus. I asked both children which they would rather do—skate or play place. It was unanimous—skating.

When we arrived at the rink I asked again, skating or play

place. Same answer yet again—skating. I asked a third time as they were waiting for skates in their sizes. I reminded them that we were there to skate and not go back and forth between skates on, skates off. Yet again they agreed that skating was their choice.

At first everything went great. Round and round the rink we went. Kelton was already quite the skater and wasted no time in skating circles around his sister. If he didn't know the words to the songs he would make them up. Brenna was still a novice but wanted to be independent as well.

"I can do it on my own, Momma."

I just walked beside her and caught her each time she'd start to fall.

Thirty minutes into our routine circles Brenna decided she had had enough of skating. She wanted the play area. I reminded her that we were there to skate only. We would do the play area on another day.

Yes, the temper tantrums started. I managed to ignore the first few outbursts. The music was loud, and I tried to focus on the lyrics rather than my daughter's wails of self-pity.

I tried to distract her, humor her, and encourage her skating abilities. I finally warned her that if the tantrums did not stop we would just have to leave.

The constant whining and complaining finally reached the point where I could not ignore it anymore.

I made the incredibly unpopular decision that we were leaving.

As you can imagine that announcement did not meet with the approval of anyone. Brenna managed to plop herself in the middle of the rink and started screaming. While hauling her over to the benches to take off her skates, I tried to explain to Kelton why we were leaving.

I did feel sorry for my son. He had been having a wonderful time. In between Brenna's screams of anger I told Kelton we could go get the bicycle we had been talking about. He had outgrown his old bike, and Geoff and I had already talked about getting him a bigger one for the upcoming summer months. In my thinking, this would be a great time to get it. The joy I expected to hear from my firstborn was not what I heard.

"But Mom, I want a toy."

A what? I honestly could not believe my ears. Here I was offering him a bicycle that would last for a year or more, and he wanted a toy. A toy he would probably play with for a few hours before putting it down in search of something new.

I tried to reason with him.

"Kelton, a bike is something you would have all year to ride and enjoy. You have plenty of other toys at home."

"But, Mom, I want a new toy."

I was flabbergasted and frustrated. Brenna was still crying, and Kelton was starting to pitch a fit. I was not a happy mom. After dropping off the skates I picked up a still screaming Brenna and grabbed Kelton, now whining, by the hand. I marched them both out to the van.

To say it was a miserable ride home would be an understatement. Both children were crying. I was so furious I wanted to cry.

When we finally reached our home I sent both children to their rooms with strict orders not to come out until I said so.

I needed a few moments to regroup, to vent my frustration due to my seemingly ungrateful offspring. I did what I usually do in those circumstances. I called Geoff. I wanted to let him know what *his* children had done that afternoon.

Geoff did what he normally does when I call in those moods. He listened. Then he said, "I love you." He didn't call me a bad mother. He didn't say I should have handled it another way. He didn't judge my actions. He listened. He said, "I love you."

During our conversation my anger turned to hurt. I made the comment that I did not understand why our son would turn down a gift that I knew would bring him so much joy for a long time in favor of a toy that would only bring short term joy.

In Sunday School the next morning I heard it . . . God's voice. I have no idea what comment was said in class that prompted it, but there it was . . . God's voice, loud and clear.

Tonya, what about the gifts I want to give to you that you refuse?

Ouch. That hurt. The reality of those words physically hurt.

As Kelton's mom I knew the bike would make him happy nearly everyday for a long time, and it would be a gift that he would appreciate time and time again. Kelton, however, didn't want to focus on the long term. He wanted the here and now. He wanted a toy. It was something that would probably break in a few days. Something he would probably forget about in a short time. He couldn't see past his here and now. His need for immediate fulfillment outweighed his need for long term fulfillment.

Isn't it amazing that we do the same thing to God? God looks down with loving eyes and says, "I have this wonderful, awesome gift prepared just for you."

"But God, I want this instead."

"But God, this is not what I asked for."

"But God, I want it now."

"But God, I don't want to wait."

God our Creator, the One who sees and knows everything, wants to give us, His children, wonderful gifts, advantages, and love beyond our greatest expectations.

Yet because we view with human eyes we don't see it. We ask for what we want now. We ask for what we can see with our limited vision. There are times when we don't even know what it is we want but we want it anyway. We want it now, not later. We want it our way, not God's way.

Just as I, as a mother, never stop wanting to give the best to my children, our God will continue to give His best to us, whether we deserve it or not. The difficulty lies in the willingness to accept God's gifts on His time schedule, not ours. If we don't see an immediate response from God then we feel cheated. We assume that because we are God's children that we have certain rights and privileges. We assume that because God loves us and wants the best for us that we have the right to know on what timetable God is working. God's gifts and blessings are ours if we choose to receive them but when we do choose to receive those gifts we also choose to trust in God alone. It's not about what we want and when we want it. It's about receiving God's gifts with a heart that is pure and open.

The question then becomes, will you accept God's gifts on His time schedule or reject them to satisfy your short term enjoyment?

Father God, thank You for loving me enough to offer me wonderful gifts of love even though I don't deserve them. Help me, Lord, to look beyond myself and look to You in order to better see Your blessings in my life.

More than Just Words: I Love You

"Love is patient, love is kind. It does not envy, it does not boast, it is not proud. It is not rude, it is not self-seeking, it is not easily angered, it keeps no record of wrongs. Love does not delight in evil but rejoices with the truth. It always protects, always trusts, always hopes, always perseveres. Love never fails."

1 Corinthians 13:4–8a (NIV)

"Hi-yah!" Wrestle time with Daddy! This rough and tumble playtime has always been an important pastime in the young lives of our two children. It started as soon as they could stand and tackle.

I have learned through practice that wrestle time with Mommy just isn't the same as with Daddy. I guess I just don't play hard enough for them!

They, including my husband, seem to live for the Tarzan-like yells, tackling grunts and a no-holds barred time of pure unadulterated wildness. I usually sit on the sidelines and cheer them on, often yelling for them to be careful or to watch out for the furniture. Of course, as you can imagine, those warnings generally fall on deaf ears.

Every great once in a while, when they are feeling generous and perhaps pity, they accept me into their sacred circle of bonding. Most of the time I don't feel left out. I know how much they all need that time together.

It was during one of those wrestle-mania nights that Geoff asked Kelton, "Do you know I love you?"

Kelton responded with the blunt honesty of a four-year-old, "Of course, Daddy. You tell me that all the time."

Geoff and I just smiled and chuckled over his innocent comment and the wrestling continued.

It wasn't until several days later that I began to actually think about the words Kelton had said that night. I began to think with my heart rather than just my head.

As a parent, I want desperately for my children to know beyond any shadow of a doubt that I love them. The love I have for them is unconditional.

I love them when the chocolate milk spills on the tan carpet for the twelfth time. I love them with spaghetti faces and ketchup fingers. I love them when they draw crayon and marker circles on the walls. When they use all the liquid soap to wash a baby doll in the bathtub while also practicing the breaststroke and splashing water all over the bathroom floor, I love them.

I love them at 5:30 in the morning when all my blurry eyes can see is a smile at my bedside. I love them when they make me so angry I want to scream.

I love reading books on the couch. I love baking, decorating, and then eating Christmas cookies. I love raking leaves in the fall, making a snowman in the winter, splashing in mud puddles in the spring, and playing ball in the summer. I love watching them play, watching them sing, dance, and revel in the joy they know as childhood.

We tell our children we love them in so many ways. Often we are left to only hope they hear our fervent cries of devotion. To actually hear Kelton say, "You tell me that all the time," was pure music to our ears. Our son was hearing and listening to what we try so hard to express to him.

Now, imagine a conversation with God.

Tonya, do you know how much I love you?

Yes, God. You tell me that all the time. Through the eyes of my children, whether tear soaked or laughter filled. I hear it in their voices, their laughter, their stories, their never-ending energy, and their love given so freely.

Yes, God. You tell me through my husband. In his support, caring, understanding, love, forgiveness, patience. In his laughter and companionship that You designed for me.

Yes, God. You tell me through my family, my Mom, Dad, brother, my grandparents. My family through marriage you have blessed me with. My friends who help me grow and become better than I was the day before.

Yes, God. You tell me through the beauty of Your world. The sunlight through the icicles in winter, the tulips and daffodils in the spring, the green grass of summer and the glorious oranges, reds, and yellows of the fall.

God shows me His love in so many ways. God's love is unconditional. He loves me when I don't feel like being a mom or a wife, when I'm tired of being responsible, when I'm grouchy and angry and jealous and exhausted!

Even though I love my children more than words can say God loves me a thousand times more! How can that be? My earthly mind cannot comprehend the enormity of that great love.

Now back to the conversation with God. Imagine standing in the glory of God, surrounded by His love and goodness. This time it is I who speaks first.

"God, do You know I love You?"

Yes, Tonya, you tell me that all the time.

What a challenge to pursue! We each have the opportunity to tell God how much we love Him. Do we turn and walk away? Do we shrug and say, "Oh, I'm sure God already knows. He is all-knowing after all."

The *Reflection* of God

We desire to let our children know how much we love them through our words and actions. We do not just assume they know our love for them is theirs for the taking. Why would we do that with our Father and Creator?

Will you accept the challenge of letting God know how much you love Him? Or will you be the one who walks away?

Thank You, God for teaching me about Your amazing love by allowing me to love my children. Please, God, help me to show You, in how I live each day, that my love is also my gift to You.

Mother + Children = Worry

"Who of you by worrying can add a single hour to his life?"
Luke 12:25(NIV)

"Hi, Honey! I have two tickets to the St. Louis Cardinals baseball game tonight. Do you want to go?"

Hmmm. Yes! Unfortunately, it was 4:30 p.m. Three hours before game time in St. Louis which would be one and a half to two hours away depending upon who was driving and traffic!

As much as I wanted to go I knew there was no way I could get a babysitter at such late notice and for what would be a late night.

Geoff tried all of his friends . . . they were working. He tried my brother but he was working, too. Just as he was about to give up and not go to the game I suggested he take our five-year-old son. It took some initial coaxing to get Kelton ready to go but then the excitement set in and Daddy and

Kelton were on their way for a big night of male bonding at the ballpark.

That left us girls to our own devices. Brenna was not happy about being left out. She and I decided we would have our own version of a girl's night out. We went to our favorite Mexican restaurant with the promise of cheese dip and steak nachos, hold the veggies, please!

We sat side by side at a table in the middle of one section of the restaurant. The side booths were no more than three feet away.

Our girl talk involved those things considered important in the life of a three-year-old . . . her friends at day care. Who said what? Who did something amazing? Can I have some more cheese dip, Mom?

We were nearing the end of our meal when an older couple walked in and sat at the booth closest to us. I caught them looking over at us several times and smiling.

The man initially tried to start a conversation with Brenna. He asked her a few questions which she promptly ignored. The woman mentioned that they had grandchildren about Brenna's age.

Both of my children are very outgoing and great conversationalists if they know someone. However, if they do not know a person or feel uncomfortable they will hide behind me or just totally ignore the person.

With Kelton, as I experienced the parent thing for the first time, I was so embarrassed that my child would appear so rude to someone.

We teach our children not to speak to strangers but then become frustrated when they don't talk to those who are not strangers to us.

When Brenna hid her face from the man, I knew why and just smiled and shrugged.

Ah, but then my cozy little fantasy world of my daughter not talking to strangers crumbled right before my eyes.

The man asked Brenna if she had a puppy, "I bet you like puppies!"

Immediately her head popped up, and she started talking nonstop about our cat.

I was stunned and terrified at the same time.

All the warnings . . . don't talk to strangers . . . with one comment about a puppy it was all forgotten.

I knew she was safe with me. I knew the man was just trying to be polite.

However, I also knew that all it would take would be a mention of a nonexistent puppy and my baby could be gone. My naïve little world where my daughter would turn and run into my outstretched arms if approached by a stranger was shattered.

What if we were at the park, the store, the zoo? What if a

stranger said she had a puppy in her car? What if she wanted to see the puppy? What if? What if?

The rational side of me knows that the worrying is natural and normal.

The irrational mother bear protecting her cub side of me worries about that which I cannot control.

I can teach my children to stay away from strangers. I can teach them to be careful who they talk to. With that said, it is also my duty to teach them to trust their instincts and to listen to the soft voices of angels in their ears. I can pray for their safety.

I can't, no matter how much I want to, I cannot guarantee their safety.

That, my friends, hurts. They are my babies, my flesh and blood, my happiness, my joy, my frustration. No matter how hard I try or how much I pray, I don't know what the next day will bring. That is where faith must step in and take over.

God has blessed me with these children. I have two choices. I can spend each second of each day worrying over the things I have no control over. Or I can turn it all to God and let Him carry the weight of my fear. His shoulders are strong enough. His heart is big enough. His promises are great enough.

As a mother placed on this earth it will not be easy to let go and give God my worries.

Just think of all the joy I can experience with my family if I am not trapped with the worrying.

Just think of all the love I can give if my energy is not drained from worry!

Father God, thank You for the blessing of my children. Please help me to turn my worries and insecurities over to You. God, please send Your grace to wash over the concerns of my heart.

I Still Love You

"People were bringing little children to Jesus to have him touch them, but the disciples rebuked them. When Jesus saw this, he was indignant. He said to them, 'Let the little children come to me, and do not hinder them, for the kingdom of God belongs to such as these. I tell you the truth, anyone who will not receive the kingdom of God like a little child will never enter it.' And he took the children in his arms, put his hands on them and blessed them."

Mark 10:13–16(NIV)

In our church, children, four years old through kindergarten, attend a children's church program on Sunday mornings. Halfway through the morning worship service the children are invited to leave the sanctuary for some activities that are geared more for their age and attention spans.

My mother's church, however, did not offer a children's church program. During one particular visit Brenna was young enough to stay in the nursery during the service but Kelton had to stay with me. For a very active five-year-old this was as close to torture as it could get.

On this very trying visit my husband could not make the trip with us. My brother, fortunately, did decide to come down and visit at the same time. My mom had to work in the nursery which left Kelton, my brother, Brad, and me in the service together.

Kelton had been attending a worship service type atmosphere for over a year having graduated from the nursery. He knew the expectations and the general outline of our services. Knowing that there would not be a children's church program to go to and that his sister was able to play in the nursery had left him with a not so worshipful attitude.

I sat Kelton in between myself and my brother. He had his church bag packed full of all sorts of goodies that would hopefully keep him quiet and occupied for the duration of the service.

It worked, for about ten minutes.

So often the church service becomes frustrating for parents of young children. Since this was not my home church the feelings of frustration were even greater. Instead of praying for the word of God to speak to my heart, I was praying that no other worshippers were about to witness what I knew would not be pretty.

I encouraged him to draw or color something. I encouraged him to look at a book. Nothing was of any interest to him.

Then the whispers started. Not the soft, trying not to attract the attention of others type whispers. Instead they were loud stage whispers.

"Mom, is it over yet?"

"Not yet."

"Mom, I'm ready to leave."

"The service isn't over yet, Kelton."

"Mom, can I go play in the nursery with Brenna?"

"No, you cannot."

"Mom, I *really* want to go now."

"I know you do."

"Mom, why don't they have children's church here?"

"I don't know why they don't."

"Mom, why is Uncle Brad here? Uncle Brad, why are you here?"

"Kelton, please use a softer voice."

"Mom, he said Germany. Isn't that the place where the army tanks were?"

At least the last question showed me that he was partially listening to the sermon!

When the answers were not what he wanted to hear he tried the ever famous crawl on the floor maneuver. The sanctuary did not have the long, bench type pews found at our church. The seats were individual pull down theatre type seats that seemed to squeak with any slight movement. I lost count of the number of squeaks that came from our section of the sanctuary.

It is quite amazing how quickly a little five-year-old body can squirm into such a tight space. I was becoming more and more agitated with each squeak of the seat and each whisper that seemed to get louder and louder.

After swiftly depositing him back into his seat I grabbed the pen out of his hand. I was going to write what I normally say when I become frustrated to the point of nearly losing all sanity.

When my children have pushed all my buttons and I feel as if I can't take any more, I stop, take a deep breath, and say I love you. It may sound silly but it has stopped me from saying many other things that I may have been feeling and thinking. It also gives me just a brief moment to remember that they are children and I am the adult. Of course the tone of my voice may leave a bit to be desired but if I can get the words out I can usually get myself under control again.

Using the pen I had grabbed from his hand and finding his notebook I wrote, "I Love You."

He looked at it for a moment and then asked what it said. Yes, another stage whisper for all to enjoy. "I love you," I whispered back.

He looked at me for a moment before a grin began on his face. It was not the "oh, how sweet" type of grin. It was not the "I love you, too, Mommy" type of grin that melts a mother's heart. Oh, no, it was the grin a boy gives when you know that something is cooking inside that little boy brain. The question then becomes, what on earth are you going to pull this time?

He took the pen from me and with another sly glance up from the corner of those blue eyes he started scribbling out the words I had written until there was no way you could see those three simple, yet heartfelt words.

Kelton leaned back in the squeaky chair, crossed his arms and looked smugly at me.

Obviously it was the reaction of an angry little boy who wasn't getting his way. He wanted in some small way, the only way he knew at the time, to hurt the one he knew loved him.

Do I think he sat there and analyzed all that in those few brief moments? Of course not, but as his mother I sure did!

I just shrugged and leaned over to him and said softly, "I still love you."

In my picture perfect world he would have thrown his arms around me and said "I'm sorry. I love you too, Mommy."

In reality he started to kick the seat in front of him. I was just about to get him up and escort him out of the sanctuary for a little mother-son conversation when my brother decided to intervene. He sat Kelton on his lap where he eventually calmed down enough to relax. By the time the service was over I was a wreck, and Kelton was nearly asleep.

I want my son to learn how to act appropriately in the worship service. The only way that is going to happen is if he attends and sits through the service. That means I'll miss out on a lot of the worship experience due to the whispers, crawling on the floor, bathroom emergencies, and so on.

There are also the worries that we will disrupt someone else and keep them from a worshipping spirit. My hope is that they either have young children also or at least remember what it was like when their children were that age!

Remember the note I wrote to Kelton? I meant every word. Even though I was frustrated to the point of distraction my love for my son never stopped. I didn't write, "I will love you only if you sit in this seat without moving it up and down and making it squeak and only if you don't make the slightest peep." I didn't say, "Oh, now you've done it. You scratched out the words 'I love you' so now I guess I just won't love you anymore."

My love for my son is unconditional. He doesn't have to earn my love. That doesn't mean that the love I offer him isn't tested and tried or stretched to the point of breaking. As human beings placed on this earth we can only love to the point that we understand love.

Kelton truly thought he could hurt me when he scratched

out those words in a fit of childish anger. Not a chance! I love him even at those times when I don't like what he has done.

Isn't it wonderful that we have a God who operates with the same mindset but at such a greater capacity?

God, I don't want to go to church today.

I still love you.

God, I don't like that person.

I still love you.

God, why can't You do things my way?

I still love you.

God, I don't want to talk to You right now.

I still love you.

God, where are You?

I still love you.

God, can You love me when I do such awful things?

I still love you.

God, I don't like the person I'm becoming.

I still love you.

God, why does it have to hurt so much?

I still love you.

God loves us always. No strings attached. No only ifs . . .

. . . only if you go to church.

. . . only if you pray.

. . . only if you read My Word.

. . . only if you're a good person.

God loves me! Wow! What an overwhelming blessing. Even at those times when I try to scratch, toss, or hide it away, God's love is still there. He is waiting to hold me, comfort me, laugh with me, and love me.

Father God, thank You for loving me when I least deserve it. Help me to receive Your love with all that I am.

Our Friend, Jesus

"Let the beloved of the Lord rest secure in him, for he shields him all day long, and the one the Lord loves rests between his shoulders."
Deuteronomy 33:12 (NIV)

I have always had a close relationship with my grandparents. My grandparents on my mom's side would often take my brother and me camping with our two cousins. Those trips were the highlight of our summer vacation from school. Grandpa Baker taught me how to fish while Grandma Baker taught me how to make peach jelly! Those memories are still precious to me all these years later.

It was important to me that my children have time to get to know their great-grandparents. Realistically, I knew my grandparents would not be around forever, and I wanted to take advantage of building relationships as early as possible.

Several times a year I would load up my two children, and

we would head to Poplar Bluff, Missouri, to visit my grand-parents. Mom would meet us there. She takes every available opportunity to see her grandkids!

One activity that my children absolutely loved involved pillow fights. They looked forward to the after dinner ritual that involved small sofa pillows.

"Great-Grandpa Baker, you can't get me!" Kelton would tease. Of course that was all the encouragement Grandpa Baker needed. They would launch pillows from a short distance and gradually get right up on each other with the intent to pummel each other with the pillows. Kelton would laugh until he had tears in his eyes.

Brenna would keep a safe distance from the main event. Every once in a while she would throw a pillow while sitting on the couch surrounded by Great-Grandma Baker and Grandma Colvin.

The pillow fights would inevitably turn into wrestling matches. Amidst the laughter there would be my voice warning Kelton not to hurt Great-Grandpa. Grandpa would laugh and say, "Tonya, he's not going to hurt me!"

I wanted to say "But Grandpa, he is four and you are eighty-six."

Those pillow fights and wrestling matches were always the high points of our visits.

The last of the pillow fights was in January 2004. During

our visit I had remembered to take my camera and snapped a few shots of my favorite people laughing and loving and bonding in their own truly unique way.

The following fall Grandpa died suddenly. We were due to go for another visit for the weekend but on the Wednesday before our expected arrival, Grandpa had a stroke.

I knew Brenna, two, would not understand, but I did worry about Kelton and his response.

After Grandpa's stroke we knew it was just a matter of days. I needed to be with my family at the hospital as they gathered to say a final good-bye. My mother-in law was going to keep the kids, so Geoff and I could head down after work on Friday.

It was important to me to be the one to tell Kelton and to try and answer his questions. I told Kelton on Thursday evening so he would know why I was gone.

He cried, and my heart ached. Even now, as I write this I can see the pain on his face and hear the heartbreak in his young voice. It still makes me cry to remember.

We talked about Great-Grandpa Baker going to live with Jesus in Heaven.

"But, Momma, I'll miss him."

"I know sweetheart. I will too."

"But we had pillow fights."

"Great-Grandpa enjoyed those pillow fights, too."

Kelton will probably never know how thankful I am that he has those memories. I am even more thankful I had a camera and the foresight to snap a few pictures so that none of us would ever forget.

Friday, while at day care, Kelton's class made self-portraits. Kelton's portrait showed two of the saddest eyes I have ever seen a child draw. When I talked with his teacher during the day she mentioned that he was much quieter and subdued than normal. When I saw the self-portrait I knew what it symbolized. It symbolized the hurt and confusion of an almost five-year-old who knew no other way to express his feelings. Again, my heart ached.

Saturday afternoon my grandpa, surrounded by his family, went home to meet the Lord.

We've had many conversations about death, Heaven, Jesus and Great-Grandpa Baker. We've talked about funerals, gravestones, cemeteries, and pillow fights. Every once in a while Kelton will want to talk about Great-Grandpa and his death. My young son has learned so much about life and death through this.

Brenna has also learned a lot but on the level a three-year-old can comprehend. She is comforted with the thought of Great-Grandpa being with Jesus.

One afternoon as we were driving past a cemetery Kelton mentioned Great-Grandpa. Brenna popped in on the conversation.

"Momma, Great-Grandpa is with Jesus, right?"

"Yes, Brenna, he is."

"Why?"

"Well, it was his time to go and live with Jesus."

"Oh, yeah. He didn't have any friends." Hmmm. How to respond? Where was this leading?

"Brenna, Great-Grandpa Baker had lots of friends."

"But he went to live with Jesus."

In the mind of our three-year-old Jesus is our friend. If you don't have any friends you go to Jesus. Interesting thought, isn't it? Maybe more people should operate with that in mind.

My grandpa, Ernest Baker, taught my children so much about life, death, and Jesus. Even though their time together was short, it still brought about some valuable lessons and amazing memories. For Kelton, he learned that age truly doesn't matter when you are laughing and loving and having fun together. He learned the incredibly hard lesson that death comes knocking into everyone's lives. He learned how to grieve.

Brenna has also learned an important lesson. When you need a friend, Jesus is there.

Yes, Jesus is our friend. Maybe if we looked at our relationship with Jesus more like a child does, our bonds might be stronger, our hearts purer and our lives more fulfilling. For many children the concept of friendship is relatively easy. They see someone they want to spend time with. They don't worry about what the other person is wearing. They don't worry about skin color or any disabilities. Their natural curiosity may lead them to ask questions but generally they don't let that stand in the way of their friendly games. Sometimes they ask the other child's name but many times the name is inconsequential. They want someone to value them enough to spend time with them.

When we, as adults, want someone to value us enough to spend time with us do we run to Jesus or do we find something or someone for a more temporal result?

The answer to that question is a very thought-provoking and personal response. Do you desire to have Jesus as your friend and all that the title of friendship entails, or are you content with getting second best?

Father God, thank You for being my friend. Thank You for filling my life with Your love. Thank You for providing a way for my children to learn of Your goodness and grace.

Terrors in the Night

"Here I am! I stand at the door and knock. If anyone hears my voice and opens the door, I will come in and eat with him, and he with me."

Revelation 3:20 (NIV)

They started just after Kelton turned four years old. We would be awakened by the cries of pain and anguish. The first few times we had no idea what was happening to our oldest child or how to help him.

Initially we thought he might be having nightmares. Through many conversations with other parents and numerous online searches we discovered the truth, night terrors.

Just the term "night terror" conjures up visions of fear and confusion. Night terrors are very different from nightmares. In the case of a nightmare the individual awakens and can often remember and relate the visions within the nightmare.

With a night terror the victim never awakens and has no recollection of the experience.

If you have never witnessed someone in the midst of a night terror it may be hard to imagine the helplessness you feel.

Kelton experiences what I have come to distinguish as two types of night terrors. One is the night terror either preceded or followed by sleepwalking. The other is the night terror where we find him still in his bed.

When he experienced the sleepwalking night terrors we would find Kelton wandering through the house in obvious distress. He would be sobbing uncontrollably. His little body would alternate between shivers and rigidity. We would either guide him back to his bed or if that would not work Geoff or I would pick him up and carry him to bed.

On the nights when he would not leave his bed I would hear Kelton calling out. Sometimes I could make out the word Mommy but most of the time it sounded like gibberish. By the time I would make it to his room he would be sitting up with his pajamas drenched in sweat. The distress on his face was bone-chilling.

Every time an episode would occur I tried the same things to calm him down. I would either sit by his side or stand by the bed. I would try to rub his arms briskly. Most of the time there was nothing I could do but wait it out. I would watch his face for some sign of my normally happy-go-lucky little boy.

During the night terrors, however, that little boy was nowhere to be seen.

Kelton would make horrible faces and grimaces. He would rotate between outstretching his arms and pointing to something in the air and then clenching his fingers into a tight letter "c" shape. The tears were real. The fear was real. His eyes would be wide open but he couldn't see me. I would be right in front of his face and there was no sign of recognition. My tears were real. My fear was real. I knew he couldn't see me but I wasn't sure if he could hear me. Sometimes I would try to sing to him but most nights I would speak softly.

"Kelton, it's Mommy. You're safe. You're in your room on your bed. You're safe. Mommy loves you. Jesus loves you. Let's lay down now." Those words became my mantra for many nights.

It seemed that if we could get him to lie down he would come out of the terror. Once the terror was over he slept peacefully. The following morning there was no memory of the events from the night before.

The time that elapses during a terror varies. The short ones last no more than four to five minutes. The worst episodes would last fifteen to twenty minutes. It was during the long episodes that I felt so totally and completely helpless. All I could do was sit with him and wait it out. Knowing that there was nothing I could do made my fear more intense. Part of me wanted to know, to be able to visually see what was occurring inside that little brain. What was so awful that it could cause my child such pain? The other part of me was terrified. I didn't want to see the terror causing visions. What if I wasn't able to get the visions out of my own mind?

The terrors have continued for over two years. They have gotten fewer and farther between. At the worst there would be a terror every night for several weeks. We would have a week or two terror free before they would start in again.

One night, while folding laundry in my bedroom, I heard a puzzle fall in the living room. The children had been in bed for over an hour, and the cat was with me. I went in the other room to see what had knocked over the puzzle. What I saw in the living room just about made my heart stop.

Kelton was standing at the front door. By the time I made it over to him he had managed to unlock the door and was attempting to pull it open. I stopped his hands and turned him around. His eyes were glassy, and his face tear streaked. It was a sleepwalking night terror. After I got him back into bed and calmed down I sat for a few minutes and watched him sleep. Peace had returned to his face. No sign of the trials just a few moments before.

When Geoff got home later from a meeting I relayed what had happened. Within fifteen minutes he had installed a safety chain at the top of the door. It was a small thing but it did provide some peace of mind.

I keep replaying that night in my head. What if Kelton had not bumped into the puzzle that night? What if he had managed to get out of the house? What if my child was wandering through the streets of our neighborhood in the dark of night? Just that one thought scares me so much that I usually stop my thoughts before they can continue. It is as if my brain refuses to think of the possibilities. For me it is a form of protection.

There are so many things we cannot explain. With Kelton's night terrors we tried everything we read or heard. We watched his food intake. We already monitored his television and computer choices. There were no major family changes in this time frame. His bedtime routine had not changed. Unfortunately, it all boils down to us having to wait the terrors out in the hope that he will eventually outgrow them.

Even though there was nothing I could do to take away the pain and physical attributes of the night terrors, I wanted and needed to be with him trying something, anything, in the hope that this time we would know the right thing to do. We wanted to protect our child from something we could not see or experience for ourselves. We needed to be near him, sitting beside him, offering words of comfort and security.

We can view God in the same way. God sits beside us offering words of comfort and security.

It's okay Tonya. I know you are hurting right now.

Tonya, let me take the burden from you.

You don't have to deal with this alone. I am here with you.

There are times when we are so wrapped up in our own little trials and daily responsibilities that we are blinded to God's promises. We lock our hearts and put up signs for no admittance. No one, let alone our Maker, is allowed to enter.

What if He expects more from me than I am able to give?

What if I can't do what He asks me to do?

How can I give God my best when I don't even know what my best is?

God stands at the door knocking. He wants to protect us from our mental terrors and fears. He wants to protect us from our own shortcomings. He wants to love us. We don't always let Him, do we?

Just as I often sit at Kelton's bedside wanting to ease the pain that he endures, God desires to do the same. He wants to guide us back to the safety and blessed security of His arms and His love.

God knows what we will choose, yet He still gives us the choice. What an honor and what a privilege! We have the choice to follow Him and receive a life of forgiveness or the choice to turn from Him. What choice will you make?

The *Reflection* of God

Father God, thank You for protecting my son when I am unable. Thank You for loving me enough to let me make choices even though I don't deserve the opportunity. God, allow me to make the choices that You have designed for me and only me.

Big Ears

"Then God said, 'Let us make man in our image, in our likeness, and let them rule over the fish of the sea and the birds of the air, over the livestock, over all the earth, and over all the creatures that move along the ground.' So God created man in his own image, in the image of God he created him; male and female he created them."

Genesis 1:26–27(NIV)

Picture Day! Like most parents I love to look at pictures of my children. When Kelton's kindergarten picture day came I was excited and apprehensive. Would he smile? Would he try to act goofy? Would my stubborn child choose to cooperate? Or does he become uncooperative just in my presence?

I knew that this was something I had no control over. The parent in me wanted to go peek and see what he was doing but the teacher side of me knew I had an obligation to my own students. I couldn't leave my first grade classroom just to go down and encourage or discourage any type of picture day play. I knew that his pictures were not something I would spend the next few years fretting over. As a mom, though, I don't always have control over what I worry about!

At last, the pictures made their way into my eager hands. He smiled! I thought the pictures were wonderful. Of course we bragged about his smile and how grown up he looked.

After several days the pictures faded into the background as the challenges and stresses of everyday life continued.

One afternoon several weeks later, Kelton and I were on our way home. Geoff had picked up Brenna so we had the drive home to discuss the activities of his day.

"Mom, a kid in my class said I have big ears."

Oh, dear.

My son has been blessed with his daddy's ears! Ever since he was an infant we would comment about Kelton having his daddy's ears. As an adult his ears will be the perfect size. Right now, however they seem a bit too big. Kelton's hair is kept very short so his ears tend to stick out more. I love his ears! They are just another part that joins all the others into the special little boy that is my son.

Geoff and I have always been careful not to make comments about Kelton's ears in his presence. We would certainly never say anything that would hurt him. Unfortunately, we don't have the same type of control over his friends and acquaintances.

Now I needed to reassure my child.

"Honey, I love your ears just as I love your blue eyes, your smile, and your energy. Your ears are just perfect for you."

Feeling a bit smug about my response I was soon brought back to reality with a bump.

"It's okay, Mom. I know I have big ears." There was no sarcasm in his voice. There was only a tone of resignation.

If you're a parent you have probably experienced that sick, gut-wrenching feeling when you know one of your babies, regardless of age, has been hurt. The hurt doesn't have to be a physical injury. The verbal assaults can cause an ache that can very nearly bring about a physical pain.

That was what I was feeling in those moments. Here was my precious, God-given gift of a son sounding so matter of fact about a hurtful comment made by a classmate. Yes, I am sure the child had no intention of hurting Kelton. It was just an observation from one child to another. It was spoken with the brutal honesty of another six-year-old little boy. However, it was *my* child who was hurt by the words.

It is so hard to reassure someone after the words have been uttered. No matter what we say to try to ease the pain, the memories of the words stay with us. Since that day in the car Kelton has never said another word about his ears or the comment made to him.

As a parent it can be so frustrating to let go of your child. We spend so much time building our children's self-confidence.

You are precious.

You are God's gift.

You are a blessing.

You are special.

God made you in His image.

We send them out into a world where words are flung around like free flying Frisbees. We've heard it so many times before, once we speak them we can't take them back so we need to be careful what we say. How often do we truly follow that advice?

How do we teach our children to live and love in a world where they will be verbally assaulted, often under the guise of humor?

"But it was just a joke."

"I didn't mean it."

"Can't you take a joke?"

"Don't be so serious."

Think about this for a moment. Imagine the pain you feel when your child has been hurt by some other child's teasing. Multiply that pain by the largest number you can comprehend. That's how I think of God's pain.

The *Reflection* of God

Can't you just see the agony across the face of God every time one of His children deals with the pain of hurtful words?

Do you wonder if He flinches when one of His children speaks words meant to harm another?

Do you wonder if He closes His eyes for a brief moment?

Do you wonder if He shakes His head in disbelief that His own children can turn on each other in the blink of an eye?

Do you wonder if He cries?

God has blessed us with so many ways to communicate with those around us. What a tremendous amount of love it takes to allow total freedom and choice with that communication. God has granted us the ability to speak, in whatever language we can, words of love and compassion, words of acceptance and caring. How often do we accept the responsibility that comes with that gift?

Father God, please grant me the ability to choose my words to bring honor to You.

Do Not Enter

"Search me, O God, and know my heart; test me and know my anxious thoughts."

Psalm 139:23 (NIV)

Isn't it amazing how a seemingly insignificant action can suddenly set us off? Age isn't a factor or a determiner, as in the case of my son.

Kelton, Brenna, and I were leaving church after a Sunday morning worship service. It was one of those overcast, windy days when the gusts seemed to come from nowhere and nearly lift a person off their feet.

Brenna had handed me her Sunday papers, but Kelton wanted to hang onto his. No words of warning would change his mind. They were his papers, and he wanted to carry them. Now mind you, any other day he would have been pawning those papers off on anyone who would take pity on those big blue six year old eyes.

As we reached the street to cross to the parking lot I reached for Brenna's hand. Kelton grabbed a hold of my coat sleeve with one hand while keeping a death grip on the papers in his other hand.

The three of us had made it to the center of the street when a huge gust of wind ripped Kelton's pages right out of his grasp. He instinctively started to chase after the papers completely forgetting that we were in the middle of the street.

I yelled at him and somehow managed to grab hold of him while still maintaining a hand on Brenna and not dropping the rest of our church paraphernalia.

I had to literally haul him across the street. His little hand remained outstretched as if the papers would somehow make their way back to his grip.

When we finally stepped foot on the sidewalk the tears started. The tears continued until we made it home, a ten minute drive across town.

The tears were not the little bits of moisture that slip out from clinched eyelids. They were also not the bite your lip and make yourself cry type of tears. These tears were a part of a full blown, totally distraught, uncontrollable downpour.

I tried several times to help him calm down. I explained that he could draw a new picture at home.

"But Mom, I colored really good on those papers," he managed to choke out between sobs.

Try number two . . ."You could try coloring a different picture after lunch."

"But Mom, those were my church pictures," he again spoke between additional sobs.

Try number three . . ."I'm sorry the wind took your papers. I know they meant a lot to you."

"Mom, a memory is all I have now." More sobs.

Ummm . . . okay. I must admit that I didn't have a clue how to continue this. It was obvious he was very upset but I couldn't help thinking they were just papers he had colored on. He could do more at a later time. I tried to nod in a sympathetic manner but I was also driving so I honestly don't know if he saw me or even realized that I was there.

Throughout all this Brenna had remained surprisingly quiet and calm. Instead of goading her brother in her usual fashion she was quite caring and concerned.

As we entered our home, Kelton, whose sobs had begun to finally subside, went right to his room and closed the door. It was quite obvious he needed his space to grieve for the lost papers.

After a few minutes of his self-imposed exile Kelton emerged from his room with what seemed to me to be an odd request.

"Mom, how do you spell 'one'?"

"One?" What was he thinking now?

"Yeah, like in 'no one can come in my room'?"

That's when I noticed the markers in his hand. My son was trying to deal with his hurt by shutting those who love him most out of the space he felt most comfortable, his bedroom.

Does that sound familiar? How many of us have tried that same thing? The cause may not be lost papers. Maybe it is a lost love, a loss of pride, a feeling of inadequacy. Maybe it is an unwillingness to believe that we are worth loving. The cause may be different for each of us but more often than not the effect will be the same. We lock down. We lock our minds. We lock our hearts. We will not allow anyone to enter. What will they see if we allow them in?

Maybe we show a physical sign like Kelton did. It doesn't have to be on paper, but it could be. A folding of the arms over the chest can be perceived as being a stay away sign.

We shake our heads in a negative fashion because we don't want to open our minds to a new way of doing things. We close our minds and say no more.

I don't want to hear what you have to say.

I don't want to have to respond to what you are saying to me.

What if I don't like what you are speaking?

What if you question who I am?

The *Reflection* of God

What if it makes me think beyond that which I feel I am capable of thinking?

Maybe our keep out signs are more of an emotional nature. Where a closed door may signal a need for privacy a closed heart can signal something else completely different. We tend to try and lock out those who love us the most. We are so afraid that if someone can see into our hearts we may not be loved for who we truly are or who we are wanting, striving, crying out to become.

A closed heart could mean an unwillingness to love or be loved. Most of us probably know someone who is so miserable they try to make life miserable for the rest of mankind as well. So many times the person who makes our lives miserable needs our love, care, and encouragement the most.

Can you imagine the helplessness and ultimately the hopelessness of someone who doesn't feel worthy of receiving love and kindness from a fellow human?

If we find ourselves unlovable how can we be willing to let God love us?

But He does! Isn't it awesome? God does love me. He loves me when I am unable to love myself.

When I wake up in the morning with no make-up and bed head . . . God loves me!

When I look in the mirror and wonder who I am . . . God loves me!

When I say the wrong thing at the wrong time . . . God loves me!

When I snap at my children or my husband . . . God loves me!

When I cannot love myself . . . God loves me!

God's love is so powerful that it can take away my insecurities. His love is so fulfilling that it can brush away my doubts. God's love is all I need. God's love is all you need. Do you allow Him to love you beyond what you can comprehend? Or do you limit God and say, "There is no way God can love me with all I've done in my life."

God searches our hearts. God is trying to get my attention. He is trying to get your attention. He has some powerful words for you! God loves you!

Father God, thank You for searching my heart and loving me. Thank You for loving me when my heart aches. Thank You for loving me when my heart wants to harden. Please God, make my heart a home for Your compassion and goodness.

But I'm the Mommy

"As a mother comforts her child, so will I comfort you."
Isaiah 66:13a (NIV)

When my youngest child was just four months old I decided to return to school to complete my master's degree in education. As a working mom I knew it would not be easy, but certain circumstances had presented themselves that made it difficult to pass up this opportunity.

The classes would be one night a week in our town. I wouldn't have to travel. A co-worker, and friend, also wanted to attend. I hoped it would be easier if I had a friend to help motivate me on those nights when I struggled with leaving my children. Tori is also the mother of two small children, so I knew that our struggles would be mirror images much of the time.

My biggest issue was going to be childcare. Geoff's schedule does not allow him to be home every night. I knew that more often than not I would have to have someone else watch Kelton and Brenna while I attended class.

Initially my mom was able to help. I felt better about leaving them with Grandma. Unfortunately, not long into the program my parents moved.

One of the workers at the child care center where my children attended was interested in extra income. I trusted Crystal completely so I approached her with the opportunity to watch my little ones one night a week. Kelton and Brenna knew Miss Crystal from "school" so I knew they would be happy. She agreed, and we were set.

There were many times I dreaded class night. Kelton, three, and Brenna, six months, were not happy that Mom was leaving. I knew they would be fine once I was out of view but there were so many nights I cried all the way to class. I could not get the picture out of my head of them standing at the door crying and calling my name.

We all fell into a routine that was at least bearable if not perfect.

One night several months later I had a house full of friends over for a basket show. Several friends had brought their children, and Geoff was keeping them all occupied playing in our children's rooms. Brenna was crawling and starting to pull herself up using any available furniture. She was showing off her newfound skill to the adults. As she managed to pull herself up the room full of moms all cheered for her. Brenna turned to see everyone and promptly lost her balance. She fell and bumped her head on the way down.

I try very hard not to overreact when one of my children fall. I don't want them to feel they must have a reaction to every little bump and bruise. I didn't jump up and run over. I simply said something along the line of "Oops! You're okay."

Brenna started to cry. It was more of an "I didn't expect to fall" cry rather than "Ow, that really hurt."

She started to crawl over to me, and that's when it happened. My baby girl bypassed me and went straight to her babysitter. I literally felt my heart break.

To me there seemed to be a silent hush that fell over the room. I felt like everyone was watching to see my reaction. Poor Crystal didn't know what to do. Brenna, still whining, wanted to be picked up, but Crystal hesitated, not sure whether to pick her up or wait for me. I tried so hard to laugh if off and told Crystal it was okay to pick her up. Inside however, I was a wreck.

The program continued but for me time had stopped when Brenna went to Crystal for comfort. As hard as I tried I couldn't stop the tears. I did manage to keep from sobbing but I couldn't keep the tears from flowing freely.

Everyone was so nice and supportive but to me it wasn't enough.

"Why didn't she come to me? She should have come to me," I asked my friends later that evening.

"It doesn't mean anything," another friendly offer of help.

"But, I'm the Mommy," was all I could manage to say at that time.

"Tonya, she knows who her mommy is. Nothing has changed that or will change that." It took the words of my own mother to get me under some semblance of control.

She was right you know. Brenna knew who her mommy was that night, and she knows today. Her crawling to Crystal was not an intentional slam on my mothering skills. "Ha! I'll show you. I fell down, and you didn't pick me up. You leave me to go to class. You're not my mommy." Brenna was nearly ten months old. She went to a person she recognized in a crowd of unknown faces.

While I took it as she thought Crystal was her mommy because of all the time she had spent with her, Brenna just wanted someone she knew to offer words of comfort.

Many times we run to other people or other circumstances instead of running into the arms of our Heavenly Father.

God watches us fall down over and over. We want that love, comfort, and words of affirmation. Do we look for God, or do we look for something or someone else?

Some people might turn to alcohol as a source of comfort. Do you think God cries, "But I'm your heavenly Father"?

Some people might turn to drugs. Do you think God cries out, "But I'm your Heavenly Father"?

Some people might turn to physical relationships. Do you think God cries out, "But I'm your Heavenly Father"?

Some people turn to work. Do you think God cries out, "But I'm your Heavenly Father"?

Some people turn to violence. Do you think God cries out, "But I'm your Heavenly Father"?

Some people sink into loneliness and depression. Do you think God cries out, "But I'm your Heavenly Father"?

God creates us, loves us, and desires the best for each of us. We lose sight of His will, stumble, and fall. Instead of turning to our Father in Heaven we go other directions.

The pain I felt when Brenna went to another woman for comfort instead of her mother, the one who carried her, loves her, and wants the best for her, is nothing compared to the pain God must feel when we turn our prideful backs on Him.

God can heal our hearts. God can heal our thoughts. God can heal and forgive, if we let Him. How often do we let Him heal us first? Don't we tend to try other methods before we try God?

We think we can handle everything but only God can truly heal and love us the way He designed us to be loved.

Why not try God first instead of last?

Father God, thank You for teaching me about Your love through my daughter. Please help me to love when I am hurting and need healing. Amen.

Hold Me

"He tends his flock like a shepherd: He gathers the lambs in his arms and carries them close to his heart; he gently leads those that have young."

Isaiah 40:11 (NIV)

"Up."

"No, Brenna. I'll hold your hand, but I'm not going to pick you up right now."

Every once in a while my almost four-year-old regresses to the language of a two-year-old by her simple request of "Up." Sometimes there are no words, just arms uplifted and a pout or perhaps a grunt.

She has reached the age and size where she doesn't get carried around by Mom and Dad like she used to.

It's often a hard concept to understand, both for the

child and the parents. When do we stop physically carrying each other?

As parents we spend so much time holding and lifting our children. Then suddenly, all too soon, it's over.

"No, honey, you're a big girl/boy now."

"No, honey, you're too old to be carried around."

"No, honey, Mommy's too tired to pick you up."

It's kind of sad when you think about it. As soon as a baby is born, it is held. No sooner does the infant make its first cry, and we wrap our arms around it. Those first few months may be a blur for new parents but one thing is certain, the child is held.

Baby cries, we pick her up and hold her close.

Baby laughs, we pick him up and hold him close.

Baby coughs, we hold her.

Baby coos, we hold him.

Watch a room full of women when a new baby is brought into the room! Most women jump at the chance to hold the new baby even for just a few brief moments.

As the infant grows she still depends upon us to carry her around and offer comfort in the security of our arms.

Then come the moments of independence. The child wants down to explore. The world is full of adventures, and a child is a willing explorer.

The older our children get the harder it is to slow them

down enough to hold them close. It seems that it is only when he is sick or extremely tired that Kelton lets me hold him now. He has reached the age of wanting to exert his need to separate. I do realize that the older he gets the stronger the need for separation will become.

As a mom, I thrive on being needed. Brenna needs a hug. I'm there. Kelton needs help learning to tie his shoes. I'm there. But what happens when I'm not needed as much as when they were younger.

I can still see the hurt on Geoff's face when Kelton told him, "Daddy, I don't need you to hold my hand now."

There was the momentary ache when Kelton informed me that he didn't need me to walk him to his kindergarten class on the second day of school. Learning when to let go and when to hold on is hard for us all. Our children included.

Just as our own children want to strike out on their own and taste the sweetness of uncharted independence we do the same with our Heavenly Father.

"It's okay God, I don't need You to hold my hand right now. I'm a big girl. Look at what I've done."

We fool ourselves into thinking that all our successes come from our own devices.

There are so many times when God is reaching down to us, and we ignore His outstretched arms.

We're too busy.

We don't want to be bothered.

We don't want to be a bother.

We feel we can handle situations on our own.

We're scared of what reaching up to God will mean.

If we reach out to God what will He expect from us?

I don't think God expects anything from us. I think He desires and wants us, but I don't think He expects anything from us.

If God does not expect anything from us then what does He want or desire from us?

God desires a relationship with us. A relationship . . . not a one sided relationship but an all encompassing, every part of us relationship.

That relationship brings other desires such as communication. God wants to hear from you about you. Just as I want my children to come to me with their dreams, fears, concerns, and questions, God desires the same from me.

I often tell God my fears and concerns but I also need to remember to share my dreams, goals, and my heart's desires with Him.

God wants to hear my questions. If I can't go to God with my questions, who then can I turn to? Only God has the answers. Even if those answers are not what I want to hear. Even if those answers are hard to swallow, God knows the answers and prepares me to handle His responses.

The *Reflection* of God

Passion is something else God desires from us. Passion for Him and for our families, for our earthly endeavors and for our churches, and for His people are all ways to reach up to God.

God desires and wants to be needed. He never gets tired of holding us. I love my children, but my arms get tired from trying to lift them or hold them for long segments of time. What a blessing that God's arms never tire. God never says . . .

I'm too busy.

You're too big.

Not now, maybe later.

God reaches down and longs to wrap us up in His arms. Are we willing to reach out our arms to Him?

It only takes that one word, "Up." If you're afraid to utter that one word, you don't have to say anything, just raise your arms to God. He'll do the rest.

Father God, thank You for lifting me when I am weak. Thank You for holding me in the security of Your arms.

Is Anyone Listening?

"*This is the confidence we have in approaching God: that if we ask anything according to his will, he hears us. And if we know that he hears us—whatever we ask—we know that we have what we asked of him.*"

1 John 5:14 (NIV)

"Where are we going?"

"We are going to the store."

"Why?"

"We need to get some things."

"Oh."

Two minutes later the conversation continues with my three and a half-year-old daughter.

"Mom, where are we going?"

"We are going to the store, Brenna."

"But why?"

"We need to pick up a few things."

"Oh, yeah."

Two more minutes pass.

"Mom, are we going to the store?"

"Yes, Brenna."

"Do we need something?"

"Yes, Brenna."

"Oh, okay."

Two more minutes have passed along with most of my patience.

"Mom, why are we at the store?"

"Brenna, why do you think we are at the store?"

"We need to get stuff?"

"Yes, Brenna."

"Hey, Mom, we're at the store. Can we get some stuff?"

By this point I am ready to pull out my hair and scream yes, yes, and yes. I really want to ask, "Do you listen when I speak to you?" "What have I been telling you all this time?" "How many times do I need to repeat myself?" I could go on and on with the thoughts that were running through my mind. The frustration at having to repeat myself over and over and yet over again can become so strong.

When Kelton, our first child, went through this I was so worried about hearing loss. Having suffered through varying levels of hearing loss myself, I was terrified that my child would struggle with this as well.

I made all kinds of excuses. Can he hear me? What if he is losing his sense of hearing? Is there something wrong with my child? How can I help him? The questions and answer-seeking continued.

The most obvious answers I chose to ignore at first. What if my child is choosing not to listen to me? Why would my child ignore me? Could Kelton have his father's gift for selective hearing?

Initially I chose to believe none of that was true. We had his ears checked. Everything was fine. We talked to his doctor. Physically it seemed all was well. Even though I was getting closer to admitting it was merely my child choosing whether or not to listen I tried another source.

I spoke with our parent educator contact. Joyce told me what I had been avoiding for months. First, Kelton is getting a response from me every time I choose to repeat a comment or request. Second, he is choosing to allow other distractions, such as the entire world, keep him from listening. He might hear my voice, but he's not listening to the words.

Yes, I knew all that. Deep down I knew my son was allowing the rest of the world to keep him from listening to me. I still needed another parent to tell me and help me understand.

It didn't change my frustration level, but it did help me learn to deal with my responses a bit.

Kelton has gotten a bit better about the listening versus hearing issues. He is still not as great at it as I would like but it is better.

I guess I had forgotten about the extent to which the repeating things would go until Brenna started in also. Even though I was right back to where I was with Kelton three years ago, I didn't overreact. Funny how we learn from our firstborn, isn't it?

Brenna still manages to aggravate me with the need for me to repeat things. Most of the time I think that she needs to feel somewhat in control of a situation in which she truly does not have control over, such as when we are traveling. Other times she gets distracted which is the case more often than not.

Yes, I get aggravated and frustrated, and the tone of my voice changes. Yes, I want to cry and whine. Yes, I want to scream, "I've told you a million times. Weren't you listening?"

I love my children even when they ask me the same question for the fifth time. I love my husband when I've asked him repeatedly to do some chore that is still left undone. But when I stop and truly reflect on these things it occurs to me that I do the same thing to God.

"God, do You love me?"

Yes, I created this world for you to enjoy.

The *Reflection* of God

"But God, do You really love me?"

Yes, I have blessed you with a loving husband.

"God, do You still love me?"

Yes, I've entrusted two beautiful children into your care.

"God, how can You love me?"

I love you because I am God. My love for you is so great and pure I sent my Son for you.

God shows me His love in all things, big things and little things. I see His love but I still need the reassurance that His love for me has not changed. That He has not taken the gift of love from me. I need to be reminded that I am still His. That He still wants me. God could say, *Tonya, I've told you a million times. Why aren't you listening to Me?* He doesn't do that. He reminds me all over again.

Just as my family needs things repeated before it finally seems to sink in I need the same from God. I know God loves me, but still I ask. Sometimes it is just to hear His voice. Sometimes it is to see the reflection of His love. Sometimes it is to feel His love envelop me in warmth and security.

Will my family ever stop asking me the same things over and over again? Probably not. Do I want them to? Probably not! I love them and will continue to answer their questions and remind them of my love. Even if that means telling Brenna four times that we are going to the store. Even if that means telling Kelton to tie his shoes as he trips on the laces for the third time. Even if that means making lists for Geoff to help him remember what I've said. Maybe they just need another reminder that I am here, that I care, that my love is still theirs.

There will still be moments of frustration and anger. Hopefully with guidance from above I will deal with it more like God deals with me, through patience and love.

Father God, thank You for Your gift of love for me. Thank You for repeating that message as many times as I need to hear it!

Another Argument

"With the tongue we praise our Lord and Father, and with it we curse men, who have been made in God's likeness."

James 3:9 (NIV)

"Mom, she's touching me."

"No, I'm not."

"Yes, you are."

"Nuh-uh."

"Uh-huh."

Here we go again. It's another argument. I knew that having more than one child would mean there would be plenty of brother and sister type fighting. I was not so naïve to believe that my children would not fall into the fighting and arguing that siblings are notorious for. However, I truly did not think the fights would start so soon.

Kelton did very well with the arrival of his sister. We were very careful to give him plenty of time to get used to someone new in our family. Even though we were obviously thrilled, excited, and exhausted with baby Brenna, we were very cautious in how we approached Kelton with the baby. We never tried to push him into a relationship with her. We gave him plenty of time to adjust and accept. Overall it worked. The transition from being the only child to being the big brother was much better than we had anticipated.

Friends and family members had warned us of what types of behaviors to expect from two and a half-year-old Kelton with the loss of being the one and only.

Perhaps that is why I thought the real fights wouldn't start until they were much older. I knew there would be disagreements and sharing issues over toys and such. I just wasn't prepared for the intentional antagonizing words of anger that poured from our children's mouths at such a young age.

Brenna's language skills have always been advanced. She was able to speak in complete sentences and hold conversations with adults long before she was two and a half. Her speech was clear, and her thoughts and opinions well expressed.

Obviously being able to speak her mind at that age meant she was able to defend herself verbally with her brother. Thus, the fighting began.

Fortunately, in my opinion, the fights are all verbal right now. I can remember my brother, who is three years younger, and I getting into some major fist fights when my parents were not around. My husband and his younger brother had many a physical blowout as well. I'm sure many other siblings have had those physical confrontations. I dread the day my children feel the animalistic need to take the argument from verbal to physical.

I try, not always successfully, to ignore a lot of their quarrels and let them try to work it out on their own. Sometimes they are able to come to some sort of a truce or temporary peace. Other times they get too wrapped up in their words and need someone to step in and send them to their proverbial corners.

One part of me believes that these temperamental outbursts are a necessary part of their growth. They need to be able to voice their opinions in an atmosphere of acceptance and support. They also need to learn how to argue. How can I expect them to have a fair argument if they've never practiced or experienced what a fair argument consists of? They need to learn that the tone of their voice impacts their statements. They need to learn the hidden rules of fighting. As their mother, isn't that part of my responsibility?

The other part of me dreads the rise of their voices indicating a new argument is brewing. I guess it's not the general arguing that I despise as much as it's the constant picking on each other with the intent to make the other person angry. It runs the range from "Brenna pinched me" to "Kelton's touching my book" and everything in between. If the fights made sense to me maybe I could understand them a little more. I am continuously amazed at how my two little darlings can go from best buds playing pretend games in the backyard to little hellions wanting to get each other into trouble regardless of the cost of a time out. Then, within ten minutes, they are back to wanting to play together again.

There are many times I think, and yes, even believe, that they antagonize each other for the sole purpose of getting a reaction out of me. Unfortunately, there are many of those times that I fall right into the trap. I get suckered into their shenanigans. In my imagination I can just see them smile at each other and telepathically express their delight at successfully drawing me into another disagreement. I am sure, at least in my mind, that they are curious as to which side I will take in the latest verbal onslaught. I suppose it's just that I love them so much that it hurts to see them argue with each other and try to get the other one into trouble.

Do you see yet where this is going? If you look at humanity, what do we spend a large part of our time doing? We antagonize others, belittling those who are different from us, quarreling, fighting, and saying things with the intent to hurt.

There are many times those feelings of anger are directed to our own families. The ones we have been charged with loving. The ones we tend to hurt first.

The *Reflection* of God

Many times our anger is directed towards those we don't know and probably will never see again. We yell at the person who cut in front of us on the highway. We shoot visual daggers at the person who took the parking spot we were waiting for. The list could go on and on.

Sometimes our anger is directed to groups of people we truly have no knowledge of. We take the little bits we know, or think we know, and then construe them to suit our own agendas and frustrations over people and events we don't completely understand.

We antagonize, argue, and verbally degrade our fellow brothers and sisters.

Can't you just see God shaking His head in disbelief? I cannot imagine God is very happy when He hears some of the things we say to each other.

Who does she think she is? That should have been my promotion.

That's my child.

Look at that guy on the street. Why can't he get a job like everyone else?

That's my child.

Those people just don't get it.

Those are my children.

Since mankind is made in God's image what makes us think we are all that different from each other? We pick on each other, pushing the proverbial buttons in hopes of making ourselves feel better about our own insecurities. Instead of loving each other, we act to injure them.

Why does it seem to be so much easier to inflict pain rather than love? Perhaps it's because love requires something from us. Where love encourages forgiveness, anger breeds resentment. Where love encourages compassion, anger breeds hatred. Where love encourages security, anger breeds insecurity.

We spend so much time trying to make ourselves feel better or look better to those around us that we miss out on God's total package.

We miss out on relationships that could make us better individuals. We miss out on seeing the world through another's viewpoint. We miss out on being loved by one of God's children. Ultimately, we miss out on being loved completely by God.

Maybe if we opened our hearts a bit more to those around us rather than trying to degrade them for being different we would find a far deeper and fulfilling God-given appreciation for all of God's children.

Father God, thank You for teaching me through my mistakes. Please help me to teach my children to love all people because You love us.

Do I Have to?

"Teach me to do your will, for you are my God; may your good spirit lead me on level ground."
Psalm 143:10 (NIV)

My four-year-old daughter is such a performer. Put her on a stage in front of a group of people, and she shines. She is not afraid to sing out for all to hear. Brenna doesn't care if she's a bit faster than everyone else or slightly off key. She sings and dances with a pure heart and out of true enjoyment.

My son on the other hand would rather fade into the background when it comes to performing or singing in front of people. Kelton's first year in the church preschool choir he knew the songs. He practiced the songs for us at home all the time. When the time came to stand in front of the congregation during an evening worship service he absolutely refused. He made it on the platform but ran down and sat with me before the music actually started. As his preschool choir leader I was frustrated. I wanted to tell him to just stand up there. As a parent I had the momentary embarrassment of thinking what will people say.

Other parents came up to me and all said the same basic things. Don't worry about it. He's only three years old. He's fine. No one minds. Don't push him. You'll laugh about this later.

They were all right. It truly didn't matter. He was only three years old, and I am able to laugh about it now.

Fast forward now three years. After a few years with no preschool choir we started up again. Having both Kelton and Brenna in the choir and with me leading it made for a few rough moments. Fortunately, the rough moments were over-shadowed by fun and singing. Our choir worked for months on a few songs to sing for the congregation on a Sunday morning. I chose songs the children enjoyed and knew the best. Brenna was so excited about singing in big church.

"Is it today? When do we sing? I can't wait to sing. Is it church day yet?"

The morning of the performance arrived. Brenna was up and dressed before the rest of the family. Kelton was moving a little slower. I knew that singing in front of everyone was not his favorite pastime. The arguments started early that morning.

"Mom, I don't want to sing."

"But you have a great voice and you know the songs."

"But I don't want to."

"You are a part of the choir, you will stand up there."

The tears started followed closely by the temper tantrums. I tried reasoning with him. I explained that a choir is a group of people and each member is important. Kelton wasn't buying into it. He kept crying and repeating that he didn't want to sing. I finally gave up the reasoning and explained that he would need to at the very least stand up with the rest of the choir. If he refused to sing that was his choice, but he would be with his fellow choir members. The temper tantrums subsided but it was obvious he was not happy about the situation.

At the very end of the Sunday school hour, Lauren, my high school assistant, and I gathered our choir members from their various rooms. Stacey, our other assistant, joined us as we practiced before the service. Everyone was excited and nervous. Kelton stood with the others through the rehearsal. I considered that to be a huge step. I had finally reached the conclusion that if he'd just stand up there and not bolt off the stage I'd be absolutely thrilled.

Following our short practice time we took care of the necessary pre-service requirements such as restroom breaks and drinks. There were nervous giggles as we made our way to the reserved pews at the front of the church. Right before we entered the sanctuary Kelton grabbed my arm.

"Mom," his voice was a hoarse whisper. *Oh, great,* I

thought. *This is it. He's going to refuse to go up with us.* Instead I was surprised by his words.

"Mom, I'll go up there and sing, but I'm not doing the motions."

I don't remember what I said to him. I remember giving him a huge hug and saying that would be great. When it was time for the Music Makers to sing, Kelton stood up on the platform on the back row of the choir. Brenna, who was still beaming at singing in big church managed to get at the front right in front of a microphone. Kelton did exactly what he said he would do. He did sing both songs and even managed a few smiles. He kept his hands in his pockets throughout the performance refusing to do the motions with the other children. Geoff and I bragged on him just as much as we did his sister.

Would I have liked for Kelton to do all that had been asked of him? Of course I would. Do I still love him even though he chose his own way of doing something? Yes, of course I do.

Do we do that to God? "God, I'll do Your will but I won't like it." "Yes, God, I'll do what You want me to do, but I'll do it my own way."

Does that sound familiar? Have you ever tried to reason with God? God, if You'll let this one thing happen then I'll do whatever You want me to do in the future. I'd venture to say that if you're truly honest with yourself you probably have.

Maybe you never said it out loud, but in your heart you spoke similar words.

Fortunately, we have a God who understands us better than we understand ourselves. He knows what we cannot voice. He knows our fears and insecurities.

Kelton did not want to sing in front of the congregation. His responsibility as a choir member was to at least stand up with his peers. I did not nor could I force him to actually sing. It was a decision he had to make for himself. I knew he could do it, but he was unsure of himself. Once he let go of a few of his fears he decided he did want to sing. The refusal to do the motions was his way of maintaining some form of control over the situation.

There have been many times when I've told God I want to do His will but then I grasp firmly to some shred of control, refusing to let myself be fully and completely used by Him.

God always provides a way for us to accomplish His will. If we are able to let go of our fears and let God take full control imagine what could be accomplished for Him. Imagine what could be accomplished in you!

Father God, please help me to seek Your will in my life. Please teach me how to let go of the fears that keep me from trusting Your will completely. Thank You for loving me enough to want the best for my life.

A Two-Letter Word

"Call to me and I will answer you and tell you great and unsearchable things you do not know."
Jeremiah 33:3 (NIV)

What is it about the word "no" that can drive a child to near insanity?

"Mom, can I have a plasma television?" queried my son.

"No." In my mind the simplicity of that one word was all that needed to be said. Kelton, however, was not impressed with the two-letter word.

"Why not?" He was not quite willing to give up on the thought of such a cool gift suggestion.

"Kelton, what would you do with a plasma television?"

"I would put it in my room."

"No," again I voiced that seemingly evil two-letter word. The tone of my voice was enough to stop the request this time.

I would think that having heard the word "no" as much as my two children have, that they would have learned how to handle it a bit better.

Not so! It doesn't seem to matter what the request might be. If the answer is no, someone has to whine or try to argue.

"Can I have more chips?"

"No." Pouting ensues.

"Can I get a new toy?"

"No."

"But Mom . . ."

"Can I go swimming?"

"Not right now."

"But I want to go now."

On and on it continues. It seems as though if one request is denied, another request is immediately voiced. No one enjoys being told no. Geoff doesn't like it when I tell him that no, I do not think he needs the same plasma television his son desires. I don't like it when I am told no, either.

As adults we have hopefully learned how to best handle our displeasure with being denied whatever request we speak. Our children don't always have that capability yet. Just as they have to be taught how to walk and how to talk they have to be taught how to deal with being told no.

This concept of learning how to deal with rejection is not an easy lesson. Each of my children handles being told no in very different ways. Kelton has just recently begun to realize that the whining truly doesn't work. As he has grown mentally as well as physically, he has started to try to debate his requests. A recent conversation showed how Kelton's mental growth is allowing him to move beyond the whining and on to other ways to try and get the answers he desires.

My mother-in-law found a kitten abandoned in the middle of a busy intersection. Having just recently acquired two other kittens she offered the tiny gray bundle of fur to us. I told Kelton and Brenna that their Dad and I would have to discuss this first. Apparently the short wait time was too long for them to wait for an answer.

"Can we go get the kitten?"

"No, Kelton, your dad and I have to discuss it first, remember?"

"But, Mom, I'll take care of it."

"Not today, Kelton."

"Mom, Arson (our other cat) could use a buddy."

"Kelton, I said not today."

"I know, Mom. I'll play with it and make sure it has food and water."

Kelton did not get what he wanted that day. He handled the use of the word "no" fairly well in that conversation. After the initial no he did continue, but the fact that he chose to use words and verbal examples rather than whining and crying was a huge step. I do not like having to explain my reasoning to my young son. In my utopia I would say no, and he would respond with an okay. That would be that . . . end of story. We all know it doesn't work that way though.

Another example is my daughter trying to have the same conversation but using the mental arguments of a four-year-old.

"Mom, I want to go get that kitten."

"No, Brenna, not today."

"But, I want it."

"Not today. Daddy and I need to talk about it first."

"But I want it now." The crying and whining start and do not end until she realizes that nothing is changing or until she is sent to her room for a cool down time, also known as time out. Generally after crying and carrying on for a while Brenna emerges from her room in search of a hug. I know that when she approaches me with the one word "hug" she is ready to make up. She needs that physical contact to reassure herself that all is well and that she is still loved.

The topic of the conversations was the same for both children. They both handled the word "no" according to the stage of development they were currently going through.

Which way do you respond when God tells you no to a request you've made? Do you whine and cry until you completely shutdown? Do you argue and question the answers you received?

My Sunday school class debated this thought not long ago. Is it okay to question God when you've received a no answer? When you ask a room full of people this question I would wager that you will receive a multitude of viewpoints, as was the case in our class. Some individuals felt it is not okay to question God, while others felt it was all right. I must admit I was one who felt it was okay. I don't know if I voiced my opinions clearly to my fellow church members that day or not. In my way of thinking it is okay to ask God why. It is okay to ask God how. It is okay to ask when and where. Now, will I receive the answers I seek? Yes, but they may not be the way I expect or even what I thought I was asking. How will I know if I don't ask?

We tell our children to ask if they don't understand something. We tell them that there are no silly questions. Isn't God our Father? Shouldn't we go to him when we don't understand something?

I do believe that there is a huge difference between asking God why something happens and questioning God's responses. I do not think that we are entitled to answers from God. God answers us because of His love and faithfulness. God answers us through grace. Having a relationship with God grants me the ability to communicate with God which does include asking why at times. However, being a child of God encourages me to trust in those answers that I don't understand or agree with.

When God tells me no I can dwell on it, cry, argue, complain and then completely miss out on the blessing that is sure to come. I may not always understand God's will but I do know that God sees the whole picture. The puzzle is complete in God's eyes. Even if I only have one piece of the puzzle and cannot discern the elaborate finished product, God can. I may still ask God why things happen the way they do, but God will always love me, questions and all.

Father God, forgive me when I feel lost and unsure of Your promises. Thank You for loving me and answering me with patience and grace.

Opera Day

"Sing to the Lord a new song; sing to the Lord, all the earth."
Psalm 96:1(NIV)

My daughter loves to sing. I'm not talking about a little ditty here, a nursery rhyme there. Oh, no, "e-i-e-i-o" is too mild for her.

At age three she started to spend entire days singing. These were not the typical three-year-old songs. She would get up on any given morning and sing her way through the day, the entire day.

Take for instance one Saturday in January. Brenna, age three and a half, woke up at her usual early bird time in a great mood. Now imagine, if you can, a little three-year-old, high-pitched, sing-song voice. If it's been too long for you to remember, just visit a church nursery or a park and sit and listen. I'm sure it won't take long before you hear little voices lifted in song. Let's go back to opera day in the Heavin household.

"Good morning, Brenna. How did you sleep?"

"I stayed in my bed all night," replied my song bird to no particular tune.

At first I thought *What on earth is she up to?* and right on the heels of that came the thought *What has she done now?* Our conversation continued, and each every comment out of her little mouth was to a new tune that she had created. Kelton wasn't too sure what to think of this at all. He kept looking at her and shaking his head in disbelief. After several hours of the non-stop songs, Kelton asked me what was wrong with his sister.

"Why is she still singing?" he wanted to know after hearing her sing a song while using the restroom.

"I guess she is just in a happy mood." I truly had no idea what had brought this about or how long it might last.

I thought that her songs were just an attention-seeking activity that would end as soon as she got tired of singing. Wow, was I wrong!

As I went through the motions of a Saturday cleaning routine Brenna sang on. I could hear her in the other room. She was playing with her dolls and singing the conversations between the toys.

"Little puppy, you have to play with me. Oh, yes, you do. You will play with my other toys." Her voice dropped to a low note as she tried to make what she identified as boy voices.

Lunch brought more songs sung with gusto.

"I love peanut butter and jelly. Do you love peanut butter and jelly? Peanut butter and jelly are my favorite. Is peanut butter and jelly your favorite, too?"

So it continued through the remainder of the day. Bath time and bedtime were both accompanied by the songs dreamed up by my precocious daughter.

I relayed the odd experience of opera day to Geoff on the phone that night. We chuckled as I tried to mimic her high-pitched little girl voice making up songs about dolls and dinner, bathtubs and potty breaks.

There are many times when Brenna's songs are a bit telling of her attitude towards her father and me. While on a family drive Brenna complained of being hungry. It wasn't dinner time yet. She had enjoyed a snack earlier but apparently that was not enough for a growing girl with an appetite to boot. Geoff and I both told her she'd have to wait to eat. Reminding her that we didn't have any food in the car didn't seem to ease her frustrations with her parents. Needless to say our little songwriter was not happy. For a brief moment there was silence, and then came the song.

"I am hungry. I am so hungry. If you are hungry you don't ever get to eat."

Geoff and I exchanged quick glances. "Do you think that was directed to us?" Geoff asked under his breath.

"Oh, definitely," I agreed.

Brenna got over her anger at us and her growling tummy. Within a few minutes she was on to another song about the cows and grass.

I love to hear Brenna's songs. They are truly from her heart and reflect her thoughts at the time. They are pure, honest, and completely her. Some of the more precious songs are the ones she sings to God. She knows the church nursery standard songs but many times she'll make up her own. She expresses her love through song. Brenna doesn't care if she is singing the right note at the right time.

How many of us worry about being on the right note at the right time while singing the praises of our Lord and King during a worship service? We refrain from singing because we are afraid that the person sitting in the pew in front of us will hear our off-key tributes.

God doesn't care if you can carry a tune or not. Some people have the gift of singing the correct notes at the perceived correct time but we all have the gift of raising our voices to praise the Almighty.

When we worry about what others think of our voices we lose sight of why we are singing in the first place. We sing because we have a God that created us and loves us in spite of our human faults.

Father God, thank You for the ability to sing Your praises. Thank You that my young daughter is not afraid to sing for You and to You. Please help me to release the fears that keep me from singing Your praises, whether it is in a church service or as I go about my daily business.

TATE PUBLISHING & *Enterprises*

Tate Publishing is committed to excellence in the publishing industry. Our staff of highly trained professionals, including editors, graphic designers, and marketing personnel, work together to produce the very finest books available. The company reflects the philosophy established by the founders, based on Psalms 68:11,

"THE LORD GAVE THE WORD AND GREAT WAS THE COMPANY OF THOSE WHO PUBLISHED IT."

If you would like further information, please call
1.888.361.9473
or visit our website
www.tatepublishing.com

TATE PUBLISHING & *Enterprises*, LLC
127 E. Trade Center Terrace
Mustang, Oklahoma 73064 USA